WINTER
Clip Art A La Carte

Concept and compilation
by
Imogene Forte

Incentive Publications, Inc.
Nashville, Tennessee

The material in this book is a copyrighted property of Incentive Publications, Inc., and may be used with permission of the copyright holder in the following manner: Teachers purchasing a copy of this book are granted permission without restrictions to reproduce illustrations for classroom use as they see fit.

For other uses, please note: No more than twelve illustrations from the work may be used in any said publication without special permission or terms granted by the publisher. A credit line recognizing the title and publisher will be appreciated whenever possible. Reproduction of the book in whole is prohibited under all circumstances. Teachers purchasing a copy of the book are granted permission to reproduce illustrations for classroom use as they see fit.

Cover by Susan Eaddy
Designed by Dianna Richey

ISBN 0-86530-201-4

Table of Contents

About This Book

The three books in the KIDS' STUFF™ CLIP ART A LA CARTE series (fall, winter, spring) were designed to meet the many requests we have had for a collection of our unique KIDS' STUFF™ art to communicate, motivate, and appeal to students, parents, and especially to teachers. It sounds easy, but you would not believe the many hours we spent adapting and thematically organizing the hundreds of publishers quality offerings in these books. The art on each page is printed on one side only to allow for selections to be clipped and used directly from the pages or for a photo copy to be made so that the books may be kept intact for future use.

The following 101 suggestions and the illustrated projects on pages 5-7 are provided to help you get started. So we invite you to clip, snip, and enjoy KIDS' STUFF™ CLIP ART A LA CARTE. It's that easy!

Activity Cards
Art Projects
Awards
Badges
Bag Decorations
Banners
Booklet Covers
Bookmarks
Book Plates
Borders
Bracelets
Brochures
Bulletin Boards
Bulletins
Calendars
Categorization
Chalkboard
  Projects
Charts
Collages:
  •Animals
  •Ecology
  •Exercise
  •Health
  •Holidays
  •Mother Goose
  •Reading
  •Safety
  •Seasons
  •Ships and Boats
  •Toys
  •Traffic
  •Weather
Communicators

Cutups
Desk Identifiers
Dioramas
Door Knob Hangers
Envelopes
Flip-Ups
Folder Decorations
Fold-Ups
Forms
Frames
Game Boards
Game Pieces
Gift Folders
Gifts
Gift Tags
Gift Wrap Decorations
Greeting Cards
Hang-ups
Headbands
Holiday Decorations
Homework Assignments
Incentives
Invitations
Jewelry
Journals
Labels
Learning Center
  Components
Library Aids
Locker Identification
Mailboxes
Mazes
Memos
Menus

Mini Art
Mini Books
Mobiles
Motivators
Name Tags
Napkin Rings
Necklaces
Notes
Party Favors
Paste-ups
Patterns
Pick-ups
Pins
Pin-ups
Place Cards
Posters
Pop-ups
Puppets
Puzzles
Record Forms
Review Sheets
Rhyme Booklets
Room Dividers
Signs
Stand-ups
Stencils
Stick-ups
Story Starters
String-ups
Student Contracts
Student Worksheets
Teacher's Records
Tokens
Tree Decorations
Window Decorations

memos
pg. 25

announcements
pg. 21

mobiles
pg. 53

DENTAL HEALTH WEEK!

AWARD

FLOSS

BRUSH

name tags
pg. 45

Jess

Zack

Nick

Writing

booklet covers
pg. 71

Science

Miss. Andress' Class

TO:

FROM:

TO:

FOR YOU AT CHRISTMAS!

TO:
FROM:

gift tags
pg. 35, 43
47 & 57

borders
pg. 45

alphabet
bracelets
pg. 75

window
decorations
pg. 73

puzzles
pg. 43

High Flying Student

greeting
cards
pg. 59

HAPPY
HOLIDAYS!

LOVE,
BOBBY

you're
batting 100

awards
pg. 31

stand-ups
pgs. 65; 69

stencil designs
pg. 57

holiday
necklace
pg. 63

paper
framers
pg. 63

Anna

book marks
pg. 19

Personalized
stationery
pg. 77

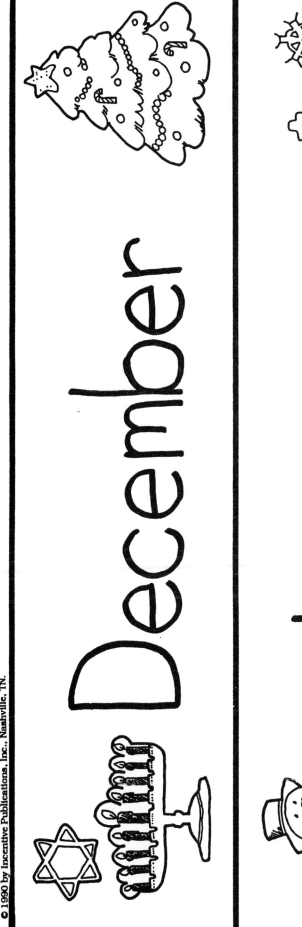

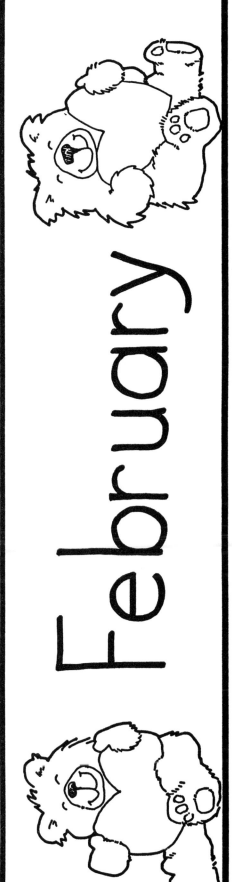

December

January

February

Holiday Helper Award

I made my teacher Proud.

School Bell Award to:

_____

is a 5 Star Reader!

COMMUNICATORS

Merry Christmas

PARTY TIME!

Happy Holidays

Happy Hanukkah

Holiday Express

DECEMBER MINI ART

CHRISTMAS

NOT A CREATURE WAS STIRRING

SANTA AND FRIENDS

HANUKKAH

TOYS

JANUARY MINI ART

HAPPY NEW YEAR

FEBRUARY

I Love you!

VALENTINE'S DAY

HEARTS

FEBRUARY MINI ART

VALENTINE MINI ART

MAIL CALL

CHINESE NEW YEAR

A FORTUNE COOKIE FOR YOU!

GUNG HAY FAT CHOY

恭喜發財

DENTAL HEALTH

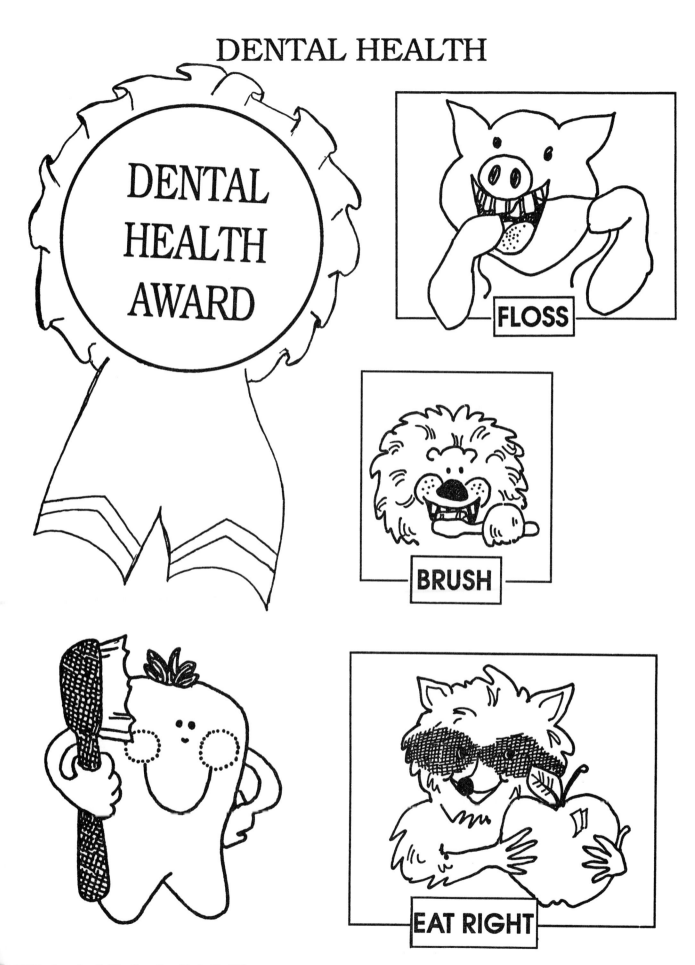

FLOSS

BRUSH

EAT RIGHT

GROUNDHOG'S DAY

WINTER WEATHER

SNOWY DAYS

WINTER WONDERS

COOL CREATURES

PAIRS AND PEARS

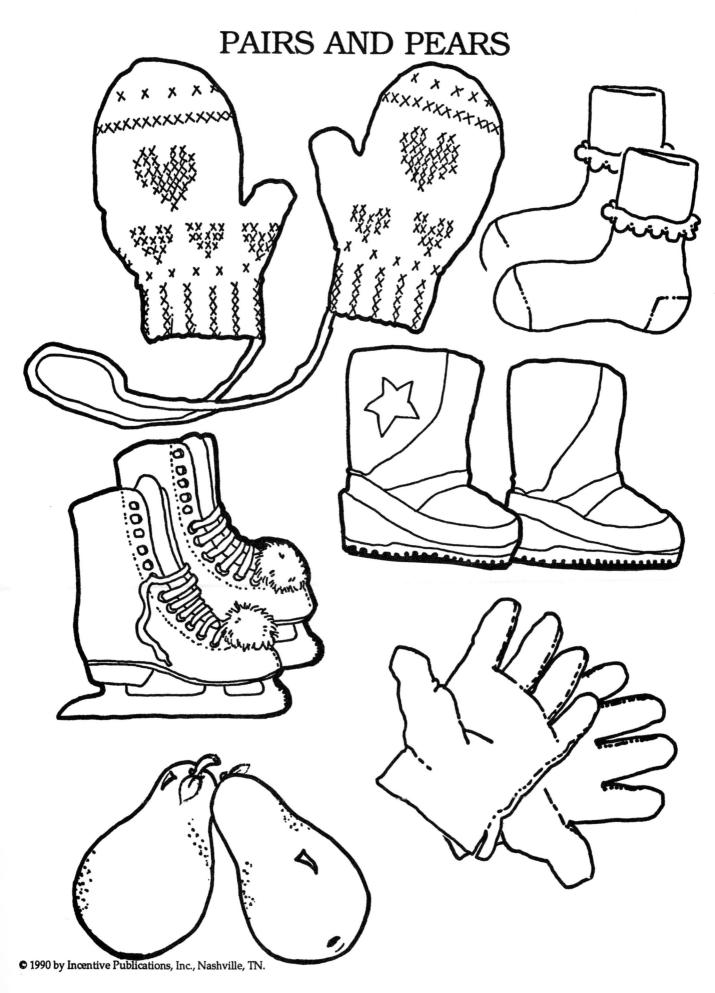

EXERCISE

JUST FOR FUN

MOTHER GOOSE